D1723912

Sailing the Secrets of Europe

Europe's Canals, by Sailboat

Another night the same... sweaty and restless, that's how I woke up from that dream that had been repeating itself several times for a long time. Always in the routine that consumes our lives in slow motion, I was very tired of it. We don't value time too much, I suppose...

I'm Gonzalo. For a few years now, I've had the idea of buying a sailboat and traveling the canals of Europe, sailing, crossing that marvelous continent with its endless history and infinite beauty.

Canals that are over 100 years old, enabling a grand journey across the entire continent, connecting the Atlantic Ocean, Mediterranean Sea, North Sea, and Black Sea – magnificent engineering feats. I needed to be breathless more often in a row; that's where life's intensity is measured.

I needed a boat that could navigate rivers, lakes, seas, and I went for it without thinking twice.

Here, I will tell you how the process has been, the good and the bad of it all. I hope you come aboard the Hummingbird and enjoy this small and humble guide – adventure and motivation – which turned into a way of life. Living our limited time to the fullest, riding our dreams...

After all, who wants to live locked in safety?

Indice

"Freedom entails responsibility. That's why most people are terrified of it."

George Bernard Shaw

Strategy

At the start of the pandemic, as we all know, we had an incredible period of reflection... the capitalist machine had come to a halt, which was perfect in that regard. This was my moment to organize everything that such an adventure entails.

With a good cup of coffee in hand and my computer, I began to explore Google Maps, mainly focusing on the Netherlands. They have excellent shipyards, rough seas, and a rich nautical culture—everything was perfect for finding a good boat with excellent sailing characteristics. It goes without saying that I enjoy visiting that country whenever the opportunity arises; I greatly admire their culture and organization.

What I was trying to do was to search for ports and within them, look for links to nautical stores, many of which advertise second-hand boats. I wasn't looking on the typical websites; they tend to inflate prices, and my primary goal was to make an intelligent purchase.

After a week of gathering data, I selected the most favorable offers on more local websites, typically not in major cities like Amsterdam or Rotterdam.

Regarding the language, nowadays, with the internet, everything is quite easy, especially considering that the Dutch speak English well too.

I want to clarify that the Netherlands is practically overcast year-round, so the sun doesn't wear down materials on the boat as much. It's also essential to note that they navigate a lot in lakes and rivers, freshwater, which is less corrosive than seawater. The Dutch, with their rich nautical culture and general purchasing power, take excellent care of their boats in terms of maintenance.

On the other hand, the high precipitation levels in the region create many fungi that can damage wood differently, so one should be mindful of that when visiting.

When looking to buy a boat, a wide range of possibilities presents itself, so it's crucial to know what kind of sailing we want to do in the future. In my case, it was more complicated; I wanted a sailboat to cross Europe through canals but also to handle maritime situations, as I am currently doing.

The most reasonable choice was a length of 9 meters (approximately 30 feet). For this length, the beam doesn't matter much in these canals, but the draft was essential. In this case, it couldn't exceed 1.60 meters, as that was the minimum draft during the dry season...

It was a bit tight, to be honest... "

Once the search for the sailboat was complete, I faced the task of thoroughly researching the most suitable route for my journey. The canal network in Europe is extensive and, in many cases, poorly documented. At this point, I encountered a significant challenge since the available information was limited.

This process turned out to be more complex than I had initially anticipated. If one of the canals I planned to traverse was out of service, had insufficient water levels, or simply wasn't navigable due to its depth, my journey would be obstructed. In this type of trip, going back to a previous point would mean losing a week or even more. Therefore, it was essential to try to anticipate and prevent such situations.

The months of rain and drought in Europe, especially in France, where the canals often ascend to higher altitudes, are crucial factors to consider. Variations in water levels can completely change the navigation conditions.

In light of this, the most reasonable option was to make a trip to the Netherlands in my van, where I could explore canals, locks, measure depths, and anticipate the difficulties I might face. However, there was an additional factor beyond my control: the lockdown in Spain, which restricted movements and posed logistical challenges.

To kick off this journey, I knew I would have to travel alone once to purchase the sailboat for various reasons. It was a smart decision to select four sailboats to view, contact their owners, and arrange individual meetings to thoroughly inspect each one. The quality of this assessment would make the difference between a successful purchase and acquiring a problematic sailboat.

With everything meticulously planned and the expectation of the end of the lockdown in Spain, I embarked on this adventure with maps on board and everything ready for the journey. Here we go!

"Survival isn't determined by the strongest species or the most intelligent one, but by the one that adapts best to change."

Charles Darwin

The Home Port of the Colibri

Purchase and Canal Reconnaissance

Loaded up the van and setting out in the early morning light from Sitges, a beautiful town in the province of Barcelona, I embarked on a journey I estimated would last approximately 24 hours, with breaks for rest, heading to Scharendijke in Schouwen, a charming island in the south of the Netherlands, where my first sailboat awaited.

Before leaving, I made sure to research the available options through one of the best nautical search engines, as well as by applying the method mentioned earlier on www.botenbank.nl, where I found a wide variety of boats from all over Europe.

Upon contacting the seller a day before my arrival, it became clear that if I arrived earlier than expected, I could enter the harbor directly and begin exploring the sailboat. The keys would be carefully stored in a designated place. This display of trust and transparency left a positive impression on me and reinforced my perception that these sellers were straightforward and honest individuals in their dealings.

My arrival in Scharendijke took place at 6:00 AM, and I immediately headed to the agreed-upon location. The boat in question was not widely recognized, as it had been built by a Dutch shipyard that had produced only a few of these sailboats. It had a polyester hull but was reinforced with an impressive amount of wood. With a length of 11 meters, it was a bit larger than I had initially considered, and a draft of 1.65 meters, which also felt somewhat tight for my preferences."

As the hours passed and I explored the sailboat more thoroughly, I decided to inspect the bilge, which is the lowest point of the boat where spilled liquids accumulate. It was then that I made a concerning discovery: there was water in the bilge. Although this water turned out to be freshwater, I couldn't help but feel wary, given that the lakes in the region are freshwater. Then, upon closer cleaning, I noticed that a frame was raised and showed significant signs of rust. This led me to assume that the sailboat had endured significant structural stress at some point, although I couldn't be certain of the details. Regrettably, I had to rule out this option.

When I shared my findings with the seller, he expressed willingness to reduce the initial price by 5000 euros. However, I understood that there were more challenges ahead, as the boat required major repairs and needed to be ready to sail within a month, which posed a considerable difficulty.

My next destination took me to Brouwershaven, also in Schouwen, where I had my second and third options in mind. Just 20 kilometers away, I arrived in this equally charming place that same afternoon, surrounded by walls that protected against turbulent waters when the weather turned adverse, a common issue in the Netherlands, as its name suggests.

The next morning, with an incredible sunrise, I met Jhap, the owner of At Sea Yachting (www.atsea.nl). Jhap wasn't merely a seller; he fully committed to every aspect of the process. It was truly fortunate to have found him. Moreover, his exceptional reviews on his website spoke of his dedication and professionalism. Watching him work to solve problems with a determined focus was a gratifying experience. Jhap was always one step ahead, ready to offer his help proactively. His tirelessly positive attitude and passion for what he did were truly admirable.

As we prepared to embark on this exciting adventure, Jhap, the owner of At Sea Yachting (www.atsea.nl), shared with me news that had both good and bad implications for my second sailboat, a Phantom 31 with a length of 9 meters and a draft of 1.70 meters. This brave sailboat, which had already circumnavigated the world, had been hauled out of the water the day before and displayed an advanced case of osmosis. This issue can sometimes generate unfounded fears, as it's not necessarily a severe threat if addressed in time. Often, it seems that fear is part of the business for some.

Unfortunately, in my case, there wasn't much I could do about it, as the previous owner was willing to keep the boat on the hardstand year-round to carry out the necessary repairs, a luxury of time I didn't have.

At that moment, Jhap handed me the keys to my third option, a sailboat from the renowned Van de Stadt shipyard, with a length of 28 feet (8.60 meters), a beam of 2.90 meters, and a draft of 1.60 meters. It was undoubtedly the best choice for crossing Europe through its canals. The Hummingbird presented itself to me, and it was love at first sight. It was an exceptionally seaworthy sailboat, and fewer than 300 units had been built worldwide. Designed by Van de Stadt and constructed by Van Heygen Belgie in Belgium, it was in excellent maintenance condition, which made the decision much easier.

After reaching an agreement, it was evident that the Northern traders took into account the Southern tendency to haggle, so I wasn't surprised that my initial proposal was low. We spent a long and pleasant day discussing the reasons behind the lower and higher prices, and everything went smoothly. My significant advantage lay in knowing that they were obligated and in a hurry to sell the sailboat, as it had been on the market for a while, reinforcing my decision to acquire it for a much lower price. Furthermore, they offered me the opportunity to use a pontoon at no cost. It's important to remember that during the pandemic, everything was practically at a standstill, although it's relevant to note that in this country, no restrictions were imposed, and masks were not required, which contrasted with the situation in France and Spain, which were experiencing understandable turmoil.

So, I stayed in the location for a while, taking care of the necessary repairs and paperwork. I decided to change the flag from Dutch to Polish and used the services of www.dutchyachtregistration.com, known for their professionalism and speed.

With this in mind, I began the return journey, aware that I would have to follow the planned route to sail once again through the rich river heritage of this continent, from north to south. In my experience, the best time for sailing in a sailboat is in mid-spring or early summer, with pleasant weather, sparse vegetation, and the rivers and canals teeming with life. In summer, conditions can become more challenging, and there is a risk of getting stuck in a canal, something I personally experienced but managed to overcome.

As the heat advances, algae can appear, which can be a problem. On more than one occasion, I had to dive to clean the shaft, propeller, and engine water intake, but despite these challenges, the experience itself was wonderful and nothing could stop it.

Left, accumulation of algae in a lock in northern France.

Below, Colibri sailing on the Meuse River, with a draft of 1.70 meters, I recall hitting the keel with some tree roots just a few miles away.

Survey and Technical Inspection of the Sailboat

In general, when we are about to acquire a vessel, it is crucial to start with an overall assessment of its condition. In this process, it's essential to pay attention to numerous maintenance details that can provide valuable information about the care the boat has received over time; there are DIY fixes from all flags.

One of the most critical aspects to consider is the condition of the hull. The phenomenon of osmosis is a factor that requires special attention. It is always recommended to haul the boat out of the water before negotiating its purchase. Sometimes, it is possible to include this process in the purchase agreement, which would be ideal. The detection of blisters on the hull and the presence of a vinegar smell in the leaking water can be signs of osmosis. In case this problem is detected, it is important to assess its severity, as it is not always as catastrophic as some claim, as long as it is not in an advanced state.

When inspecting the hull, it is necessary to pay attention to other key elements such as the propeller, which should be free of obstructions, firm, and without stains. The rudder should also be evaluated in terms of its integrity and operation. If the boat has a keel, it is important to check the bolts inside and ensure they are free from rust.

Regarding the deck, it is essential to look for cracks and possible leaks, especially if the boat contains wood in its structure. Additionally, the condition of the non-slip surface should be checked, as well as the block and fixed stanchions.

The rigging deserves special attention, making sure that it is taut and free of broken wires, and the turnbuckles should be free from rust. The mast should also be thoroughly inspected, paying attention to the base for cracks and ensuring it is upright. Fixed spreaders are an important point to verify.

The stays and backstay should receive the same attention, and the boom should not show signs of corrosion. When examining the sails, the genoa furler should move smoothly, and the condition of the lines and the sails themselves should be checked.

Regarding the steering, it should be free of play, smooth in operation, and have minimal play. The winches should turn naturally with their characteristic sound.

Inspecting the anchor well involves checking the chain and windlass if present. The seacocks should open and close smoothly, which is critical for safety in the water.

The engine deserves thorough attention. Oil or diesel leaks should be sought, and the presence of rust should be checked. Starting the engine when cold is an excellent way to assess its overall condition, paying attention to aspects like smoke, vibrations, and unusual sounds. Additionally, it should be verified that the belts are tight, the engine bed is solid, the exhaust pipe is free of rust, and the wiring is in order. The bilge is also critical; it should be dry, and if there is water, it is important to determine whether it is freshwater or saltwater.

The galley and the bathroom are important areas to evaluate, ensuring that they function correctly, and that the water supply and drainage systems are in good condition. Seals and hoses should be checked, as well as seacocks.

In the realm of electronics, it is essential to check that all onboard systems work correctly. This includes verifying the batteries and their charge, as well as inspecting all the wiring to ensure it is in order. A battery with a voltage of 11.80v is considered unusable.

Last but not least, it is crucial to dedicate enough time to the boat visit, at least five or six hours, or even more. A thorough and unhurried assessment is essential. If the person selling the boat does not allow this comprehensive inspection, it is a reason to doubt the transaction. Approaching the purchase of a boat with the right focus is fundamental, as otherwise, it could result in a costly and problematic investment.

"From a very young age, I had to interrupt my education to start going to school."

Gabriel García Márquez

Beginning of the Adventure

The Rhine River, a European river gem, stands out as one of the continent's major watercourses and constitutes the most significant aquatic artery in the European Union. This majestic river stretches over an impressive length of 1230 kilometers, opening its waters to navigation over a span of 883 kilometers, extending from Basel, Switzerland, to its grand delta, which gracefully flows into the North Sea. During its journey, the Rhine carries an imposing average flow of around 2100 cubic meters per second and gives life to a delta shared with the equally illustrious Meuse River. Among the renowned and historically significant cities that grace its banks, we can mention Basel in Switzerland, the elegant Strasbourg in France, the historic Cologne, the vibrant Düsseldorf in Germany, and the dynamic Rotterdam in the Netherlands, all silent witnesses to centuries of history flowing with the waters of this majestic river.

However, navigating these waters is neither an easy nor a light task, and in my case, I yearned to embark on this journey solo, a challenge that, I must admit, turned into an odyssey filled with obstacles. The lack of adequate and precise information led me to make mistakes and harbor countless doubts. In hindsight, I can only discourage solo navigation in the channels of this river, as the need for additional hands becomes evident at every twist and turn. Risks increase, and any error could result in collisions with the rocks surrounding these waters.

Undoubtedly, shared experiences in this environment are significantly more rewarding. True happiness, as is well known, multiplies when shared. In my case, during the first week, a former colleague was kind enough to accompany me, which proved to be invaluable. The importance of having someone with basic navigation knowledge became evident as I had to provide lessons on the go.

One should not underestimate the dangers that lurk when crossing canals and rivers; in fact, these seem more unpredictable than the challenges of the ocean. Now I find myself in the port of Jachthaven Brouwershaven, and at 8 in the morning, we will be facing the crane to unstep the mast, a maneuver to lower the mast.

With the invaluable support of the staff, we approached this task with determination. It is highly recommended to establish a sturdy foundation to support the mast, as can be seen in the attached image: solidly interlocked wooden beams. The importance of placing a beam in the center is undeniable, as the mast could be compromised, or even the integrity of its structure jeopardized.

Furthermore, it is essential to precisely mark the location of all disassembled connections, such as the rigging, satellites, and backstay. For this purpose, we suggest taking meticulous notes in a notebook, capturing detailed images, or even using nail polish to mark the nuts, a clever strategy that facilitates the task in the future. Considering that we will face a journey of approximately 76 days, during which countless events will unfold, it is imperative to be prepared. During this time, we will once again experience that youthful feeling of being 18 years old, a rejuvenation that promises a great adventure ahead!

Organizing the mast takes us a few hours, a process that we execute skillfully thanks to the professionalism of the Jhap team. After this task, we decide to head to the supermarket and fill our water and gasoline tanks to the maximum.

When we finally cast off the moorings, we experience a feeling of liberation that intoxicates us. There were countless questions that still awaited answers on our journey. This starting point marked our mile zero, the threshold of a journey that would take us through diverse languages and cultures. We felt great excitement for the adventure that lay ahead. We immersed ourselves in deep silence, anticipating any eventuality, aware that uncertainty is the very heart of adventure.

We cautiously approach the entrance of the harbor, where a motion detector immediately activates, indicating to us with a traffic light that everything is preparing to open the gates and allow us to continue our journey. After a few minutes of anticipation, we rev up the engine to 2400 revolutions per minute. We were ready to begin our ascent of the Meuse River, which in this region was part of the vast delta of the famous Rhine River. At this point, the currents were not yet a significant factor, but the area was densely marked due to the shallow waters that characterize this region. Here, natural life seemed to flow in a unique way in the world, offering a glimpse of a wild Europe that seemed taken from a dream. It was at this moment that the depth sounder became the most valuable and used instrument on board, as even with a draft of only 1.60 meters, the alarm would sound in some places, a signal that, over time, we had to learn to ignore to avoid becoming paranoid.

Navigating northeast, we headed towards our first lock, which involved an ascent of no more than one meter. The feeling of uncertainty washed over us. How is this maneuver performed? We wondered. It was essential to observe the more experienced travelers in the area, who possessed techniques we could learn from, and also keep in mind that in this region, the use of canals was common, so we would rarely be alone on this journey.

Now, allow me to explain how the traffic lights work in these waters, although it's worth noting that there may be variations depending on the country. In the Netherlands and Belgium, the gates are automatic, and in most cases, there is no need to contact them via VHF radio. In general terms, the traffic lights take on a triangular shape:

Red: Indicates that passage is not allowed.
Green: Signifies that passage is permitted, and the way is clear.
Orange: Indicates that the lock is in operation. It's important to maintain a minimum distance of 30 to 40 meters, as when it opens, vessels from the opposite side may emerge.
Double red: Indicates that the lock is out of service or malfunctioning, a situation that can occur somewhat frequently, especially in France.
Red and orange: This traffic light prepares you to enter the lock.
This information is essential to ensure safe passage throughout our exciting journey on these European rivers and canals.

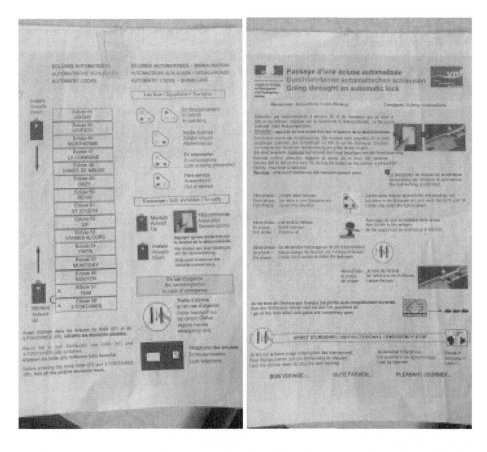

These images I'm sharing are from VNF, the company responsible for the locks in France. Although locks can vary in appearance, in France, they provide you with a remote control to activate them, and we will delve deeper into this process when we reach French territory.

Regarding navigation, I want to make some useful recommendations. First and foremost, it is highly advisable to have a physical road map on hand and mark your routes and points of interest on it. This will give you an overview of your journey and help you plan ahead.

Additionally, there is an application called Maps.me that is invaluable for navigators. This app allows you to download maps for any country and use them without an internet connection. This is especially useful because during this journey, you will find that opportunities to refuel are limited. You will need to look for gas stations near major roads and make sure you have a cart and containers for transport, as this is crucial for your journey.

OpenCPN has also been a very useful tool for us. This navigation platform provides access to free cartography, which makes planning and navigation easier. During the journey, it's important to stay attentive and regularly consult nautical charts, as there are numerous canals and junctions you need to be aware of.

Once in the region, you'll discover that navigation is very intuitive, and the canals are well marked, allowing you to enjoy a relatively worry-free journey. The combination of these tools and tips will provide you with a smoother navigation experience and allow you to focus on enjoying every moment of this exciting journey.

Our first lock in Bruinisse, completely automatic. It was there that we realized that on this journey, fenders (boat protections) would be essential, and we managed to get a few more of large size. Our sailboat is on the other side; we are already proceeding with the mast down.

A typical canal in Amsterdam.

When we passed through the first lock, we experienced a transition that was smooth and truly awe-inspiring. We only moved about half a mile before reaching the second lock, where we found ourselves ascending three meters. What was intriguing was the number of boats eagerly awaiting their turn to enter. When the traffic light turned green, everyone rushed to enter, causing some momentary chaos. It's worth noting that if you don't manage to enter a lock at that moment, you'll face the wait for the filling and emptying of water to be completed, a process that could take at least an hour. We were the last to enter, and some boats were left outside. At that moment, I realized that it's not exactly pleasant to moor your boat just two meters from the gate, as the turbulence was considerable, and our sailboat seemed to be dancing on the water. It was an initial scare, but when I looked up, I saw travelers and sailors from other boats sharing stories and enjoying that beautiful moment. It was truly wonderful.

It's important to emphasize the need for quality fenders and appropriate ropes for mooring, but it's essential to remember never to tie them tightly, as if they snag, they could jeopardize the safety of the boat or leave it in a compromised position. With these concepts in mind, all that's left is to open a delightful Belgian beer and savor the splendid scenery.

The periods inside the locks, once everything is in order, are extremely pleasant. In this case, as we ascended the Rhine River, the horizon gradually transformed, accompanied by magnificent weather. During this stage, it is essential to pay attention to the line, as the sailboat loosens it as it rises. The start of the lock maneuver is always marked by a very interesting alarm, creating an atmosphere of alertness and beauty in its surroundings.

If there are numerous vessels, they tend to cluster along the wall, giving priority to the larger ones, especially passenger vessels. These large vessels assume that other boaters already know this hierarchy and therefore enter without the need for prior consultation. During those times, it is advisable to stay out of their way and allow them to proceed unhindered.

At this moment, we are navigating through spacious water areas with a width of up to 200 meters and adequate depth as we leave the delta. However, it is noteworthy how maritime traffic is experiencing an increase both in terms of volume and the size of vessels. This evolution is highly intriguing. Additionally, it is important to note that the currents are increasing in speed, reaching up to 1.5 knots.

Here we can see a large river cruise ship and the stern of the Colibrí, with a much-needed canopy, as precipitation levels are high in that area. Highly recommended.

It's worth mentioning the remarkable flatness of this region, which includes the Netherlands, Belgium, and Luxembourg. Due to this, the canals are long and straight, perhaps somewhat monotonous in terms of scenery, but they are full of life, with rich wildlife and beautiful flora that thrive along their banks, although this can sometimes be a minor inconvenience.

In general terms, the waters in the Netherlands often have an unpleasant brownish color for swimming, and it's undeniable that in these countries, you can perceive authentic countryside aromas, pleasant at times and unpleasant at others. These smells, which may be perplexing at first, are often an integral part of the canal navigation experience, reminding us of these nations' close connection to agriculture and the natural environment.

Throughout the territory of this first country, you can find large locks, all of which are operated automatically, and the largest of them lifted us about 5 meters in height. The operation of these locks is usually flawless, thanks to the presence of sensors that efficiently activate the mechanisms. It's advisable to choose one side of the boat, for example, the starboard side, to place most of the fenders, leaving some on the port side as a precaution. When evening falls, the canals often close, so it is not advisable to navigate them at night due to the presence of numerous obstacles, even if they are properly marked.

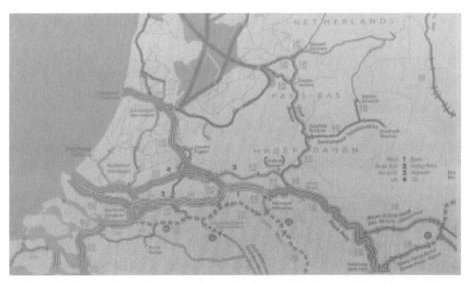

The initial stretches of ascent, the Rhine River (Rhein) and the Meuse River (Meuse).

Always, you can find a suitable dock or shoreline to spend the night. We carry two large stakes and ropes on board that allow us to moor the sailboat on the rivers' or canals' banks if we don't find a port in time. It's important to mention that, in general, we didn't have to pay for mooring anywhere, as it is uncommon in these countries to charge for this service. However, it's important to note that services may not be available at these locations, so one must be prepared, and if you find yourself in a village, it's advisable to look for gas stations or freshwater supply points. For this reason, I suggest bringing the previously mentioned guides and maps to plan the journey properly. Additionally, it's an excellent idea to carry provisions of food and drinks, as in certain remote areas, it can be challenging to find stores or restaurants.

In summary, navigating the canals of the Netherlands, Belgium, and Luxembourg is a fascinating experience that offers both challenges and rewards. The flatness of the terrain, the diversity of wildlife, and the history of river navigation in this region make each trip unique and memorable.

Felix, the companion, in control of the bow.

Dutch lock, with its ladder and openings for passing lines.

Above, the wind farms, one of many, a marvel of navigation.

To our left, the pleasure trip is crystal clear, and nothing is more intense than good silence.

All the boats moored and securely fastened, needless to say, the use of life jackets is mandatory, and in some situations, they don't start the lock until everyone has a life jacket on.

Here we had to spend the night, a very good place for it. We arrived late, and the lock was already out of service.

My intention here is to show you the bridge signals. On the left, the two yellow triangles indicate the passage, which can also be represented by lights. If one triangle is black, it means a shallower draft.

Below, you can see a sign on the red, white, and red bridge. That means passage is prohibited. In the opposite direction, we might be able to pass through there, or not.

The Meuse River, a prominent European river in the North Sea basin, originates in France and, after flowing through Belgium and the Netherlands, empties into the shared Rhine-Meuse-Scheldt delta. With a length of approximately 950 kilometers and a basin covering over 36,000 square kilometers, the Meuse stands out for its significance in the region. Its average discharge is around 400 cubic meters per second, and its basin is home to approximately nine million Europeans.

The Meuse originates in northeastern France at a modest elevation of just 409 meters above sea level. Initially, it flows northward, then changes direction to the northeast as it crosses the Ardennes massif, and finally veers westward. Its mouth is located at the Haringvliet, an entrance to the North Sea, where it divides into several branches, many of which are currently unused, creating an extensive delta.

As can be seen in the photographs, there are few sailboats that venture to sail without masts. We are a minority who choose to explore the interior of the continent, enjoying the journey along the river. Before reaching the city of 's-Hertogenbosch, we decided to explore its interior and take a shortcut by following the Zuid-Willemsvaart canal. Although these canals may seem straight and monotonous compared to other landscapes, they provide us with the opportunity to sail more peacefully and with less traffic. At these moments, we are forging a deeper connection with our sailboat and appreciating the beauty of the canals and locks.

Our journey continues at an average speed of 5 knots, and it's evident that in these canals, the currents are gentle, which is a relief when sailing against sea level. We will soon pass through Helmond, heading towards the famous city of Maastricht, which promises to be an exciting stage in our journey.

We have a green light to enter the lock, all to ourselves.

Above, as we can see on the lock wall, there is always a ladder, which I recommend having nearby. Needless to say, it is prohibited to tie yourself to it. When mooring the sailboat, you should climb it and pass a line through the highest bollard possible. I mention this because if it's an automatic lock, they won't wait for you, and before the water starts entering, you should already be on the boat. There can be a lot of turbulence (you can see the bollards in the gaps), and it's absolutely prohibited to tie them, which could be very dangerous. In this case, we have a line at the stern and another at the bow. As we go up, we will release them and, when leveling, we will quickly have to pass the line through a higher bollard.

Above, classic cargo traffic in this area, large drafts with shallow draft, they always have priority.

To the left, many swans come to greet us, or rather, many humans feed them... I've never seen such a beautiful animal with such a bad temper; it's normal for them to try to peck at you.

As we exit the Suid-Willemsvaart canal, south of the beautiful city of Roermond, we once again encounter the waters of the majestic Meuse River. However, at this point, we enter the W. Juliana canal, a section that will take us towards the charming Maastricht. This stretch of the journey is characterized by its picturesque surroundings but also by a notable increase in river traffic. At times, we begin to notice the currents against us, a challenge that adds excitement to our journey. Despite the current, the waters still maintain their dark color, indicating that aquatic vegetation is still scarce in this region.

It's impossible to navigate this area without remembering the terrible events that occurred just a few months ago. Belgium and the Netherlands were hit by one of the worst floods in their history, with a tragic death toll and a large amount of vegetation swept away by the relentless waters. As we move forward, we can't help but notice the striking mounds of dead trees piled up next to the locks. This desolate landscape reminds us of the importance of maintaining strict control over our bow, as we never know when we might encounter unexpected situations.

The water depth also begins to raise some alarms on our depth sounder, indicating that we are gaining altitude. Although we are sharing these waterways with large vessels, it is essential to remember that, despite their imposing size, these ships have a much shallower draft than practically any sailboat. This circumstance obliges us to maintain constant vigilance and to be cautious in our navigation, carefully choosing our routes.

The W. Juliana canal meanders around the city, offering us the opportunity to find essential supplies such as water and diesel fuel. It is surprising that these services are not more readily available on the riverbanks, given the amount of traffic flowing through these waters. However, this may be an opportunity to refuel at gas stations, which is possibly more cost-effective and ensures higher-quality diesel due to higher turnover. In conclusion, our journey through these waters not only immerses us in a unique natural beauty but also presents us with challenges and reflections on the interaction between nature and technology in modern navigation.

"Do not allow anyone to tell you your worth. You are the only one capable of knowing your own value."
Muhammad Ali

Entering Liège

Beautiful cityscape by the river, you can also see our temporary masthead light.

These spots like this are highly coveted for a good rest and very accessible for refueling or provisioning.

New stage, Belgium and northern France.
Meuse River and the Eastern Canal in France.

Despite enjoying the full summer, the nights in this place were characterized by their pleasant coolness, which led us to strongly recommend bringing coats and rain jackets on our nightly excursions. It was coffee time, a sacred moment we experienced with a different backdrop each day. This ritual became exactly what I had been craving: savoring the aroma of a simple coffee in a variety of landscapes, a kind of soul-soothing sustenance.

We found ourselves on the threshold of Belgium, a country that, despite its compact size, radiated a unique charm. Here, navigation took on an even more intriguing nuance, with currents that, in extreme circumstances, reached speeds of up to 3 knots. Additionally, numerous locks awaited us, and not all of them operated automatically. At times, it was necessary to make a VHF radio call to coordinate our passage. It's worth noting that the lock system in the Netherlands and Belgium is publicly accessible and free, with staff always present to ensure everything went smoothly. In each lock, there was a red button we could press in case of any issue, and in the blink of an eye, someone would be there to assist us. If the official was at a certain distance, they would respond through a microphone. In general, when pressing that button, there was always someone willing to come to our aid quickly and efficiently.

As we progressed, we noticed that the locks started to become more compact, and the river waters and canals became clearer. With the progression of daylight, life flourished around us. Small challenges arose: every few miles, we needed to reverse to free the plants that had tangled with the keel, resulting in a surprising speed boost of 2 knots. This marked the beginning of a new phase in our exciting journey, and in hindsight, I would strongly suggest bringing snorkeling gear on board the sailboat, as the region promised fascinating aquatic discoveries at every stage of the way.

The river remained our faithful guide to our destination, despite the persistent upstream current that constantly challenged us. Our beloved Hummingbird, with its Mini Sole engine running at 3400 revolutions per minute, patiently helped us move forward, covering miles upon miles in this thrilling odyssey. Over time, the first mountains began to appear on the horizon, eliciting a sense of awe in us that, although palpable, had not yet reached its peak; that would come later, in the most awe-inspiring part of our extensive journey.

At this stage of the journey, local supermarkets stood out for offering a wide variety of beers, an experience I would undoubtedly recommend to any traveler looking to fully immerse themselves in the local culture.

*Bélgica, river
Meuse.*

In Belgium, along the Meuse River, we noticed a greater number of docks lining the riverbanks, providing us with the opportunity to dock comfortably and seek out picturesque terraces where we could engage in conversations with the locals and listen to their fascinating stories.

It is worth mentioning that, according to the locals, we were the first sailors to cross these waters after the pandemic period, a fact that filled our hearts with satisfaction. People showed a sincere interest in interacting with us, eager to learn more details about our journey. As we shared our experiences and anecdotes, we noticed a special sparkle in the eyes of some, a sparkle I had experienced myself before and had been the catalyst for my decision to leave the alluring comfort of the system and shape a fuller and more rewarding life. We are all aware that time, ultimately, is synonymous with freedom.

However, being the first to resume navigation after the pandemic also came with its challenges. The maintenance staff had not worked for a long period, which was evident in the difficulties that arose with each mile traveled. This situation reminded us of the importance of meticulous planning and the need to constantly adapt to changing circumstances on our journey.

Classic Ferry, Belgium.

Medieval fortress, surely we would have been received differently 100 years ago...

Meuse River, cargo traffic on the port side, at a fork.

Who wouldn't be gazing with such fascination? Meuse River.

Frangee Bridge, Engineering Art. Meuse River, Liege - Belgium.

Belgium, what a beautiful country to explore. At this stage of the journey, the interior climate began to make itself felt, especially being near the river. In the evenings, the coolness and the morning mist enveloped you, creating a unique atmosphere. Waking up and following the scent of freshly baked bread to find our breakfast was a delight. It was as if we were tracking our first meal of the day with our noses, anticipating a good cup of coffee to kickstart our adventurous days.

At this point in the journey, our companion Félix had to leave us due to medical issues, and we continued further towards less populated areas. Somehow, this was the original idea, just Colibrí and me against the challenges of the river and navigation.

Navigating the locks solo could be challenging, but I've always enjoyed the challenges life presents us. At the start of each day, we performed a thorough check of the gasoline and ensured the engine was in perfect condition, monitoring temperatures, cooling, and oil levels. It was here that I realized the water filter frequently got clogged. It was understandable, as we were in a river, so I learned to check this component more regularly. Throughout the journey, I dismantled and cleaned the water filter more than 15 times; it became a routine I followed every three days or so.

We divided navigation into three-hour shifts at the helm, and when it was time to eat, either of us took charge of preparing something delicious. Sometimes we made stops to enjoy our meals, but our journey was long, and our goal was to reach France by the end of the rainy season. South of Belgium, we noticed that water was becoming scarce, and I estimated that the locks filled up in about 25 minutes. If the water was even scarcer, it could take a bit longer. By making these calculations, we could plan how many locks we would cross in a day, considering the increasing distances as we ventured further inland.

Our next stop was Dinant, the last town before crossing into France. Dinant was simply a dream come true and one of the most beautiful stretches of our journey. Everything in this city seemed like a symphony of natural and architectural beauty. We stayed there for several days, soaking in its magic. Sometimes, words cannot fully capture the beauty of a place, and that's when photographs can do justice to the experience we shared in Dinant.

"If with all you have you're not happy, with all you lack you won't be either."

Erich Fromm

Dinant

Left, Collégiale Notre-Dame de Dinant, a XIII-century church.

Charlemagne Viaduct, Meuse River, returning to the Colibri after buying breakfast.

Rocher Bayard, whims of nature.

Collégiale Notre-Dame de Dinant from the XIII century, in Gothic style, with a pear-shaped bell tower.

Palaces on the outskirts of Dinant.

Lock for entering Dinant, we have a green light.

This is how the ports and docks are on the river, utmost caution in the draft!

Our next stop would be Givet, a place that marked the border between Belgium and France. Here, we had to carry out an important procedure: acquire a navigation permit from VNF, Voies Navigables de France. Although they had a website, we decided it was better to go to the office in person, which is located at any border point in the country. Upon arrival, we went to the administration office, where they explained a significant change in the operation of the locks.

Up until that point, we were accustomed to automatic locks, but we were informed that it was no longer the norm in France. Now, the pass we purchased was valid for a period of time. In our case, we opted for a one-month and ten-day pass, which I calculated would be sufficient to cross all of France. However, in addition to time, they also took into account the length and width of our vessel to calculate the cost. In my case, this resulted in a payment of approximately 130 euros. In exchange, they provided us with a special remote control that we had to use when approaching a lock. However, there were also manual locks for which the remote control was not required.

The issue of the remote control turned out to be an interesting challenge. As we traveled through different regions of France, we had to switch our remote control for a region-specific one. Technology is amazing when it works, but at times, it put us through some hardships as we had one remote that malfunctioned and another one that ran out of battery at inconvenient moments. As an additional measure, they provided us with a document containing the dates and authorization number, which we had to keep visible in case of inspection.

This process added a new level of excitement and challenge to our journey through the French canals, but it also gave us the opportunity to learn and adapt to the peculiarities of navigation in this beautiful region.

"Go to school. Study. Get a job. Work. Pay taxes. Get married. Have children. Get a mortgage. Watch TV. Follow fashion. Take out loans. Act normally. Buy lots of things. Walk on the sidewalk. Choose between this product or that one. Save for when you're old. Obey the law, and above all, never question what you've been told to do. And now, repeat after me: I AM FREE!!!"

George Carlin

Beautiful landscape on the way to Givet, sailing on the Colibri.

Same lock, stern to bow; these were common in France.

"The pursuit of safety to avoid risk is the most dangerous thing we can do."

Robert T. Kiyosaki

Meuse River, heading south to Givet.

We left Dinant very early, just as the fog began to lift enough to allow us to continue our journey. At this point in the trip, the landscape had already undergone a noticeable transformation. The imposing mountains rising around us created an impressive backdrop, and the locks we encountered on our way were notably smaller than the ones we had seen before.

We had decided to turn off the sonar alarm as its constant buzzing was driving us a bit crazy and not allowing us to fully enjoy the trip. We assumed that we might encounter some scratches on the boat's hull, but we weren't overly concerned about it. Instead, we were entirely focused on following the signage and, above all, understanding the river's geography. We learned, through experience, that when taking a curve, it was best to approach the opposite side of it, as theoretically, the river had eroded more terrain at that point. This intuition and constant adaptation to the river's conditions became essential for our journey, and we adopted a truly Darwinian approach to our navigation.

This border stretch of the journey also provided an excellent opportunity for us to evaluate the best canal options for our navigation. We discovered that there were several possible routes and numerous channels to explore. The information we gathered was invaluable; it informed us about areas that had experienced heavier rains and those that had been drier. Our chosen route alerted us to the need to pick up the pace if we wanted to pass through the higher part of the river near Espinal, where the draft was already reaching 1.80 meters. Although this seemed like a tight fit considering our estimated arrival in 15 days, we decided to embrace the adventure without fear of what might come. If we couldn't make the crossing, we would resign ourselves to an unexpected and extended three-month vacation in the region without moving our boat. However, my greatest concern at that moment was the cold awaiting us in the coming weeks.

After a pleasant exchange with our French guides and completing all the necessary payments, the most experienced guide approached me and made an unexpected revelation. Throughout the pandemic, no one had properly cleaned the canals, and he warned us that we might encounter a considerable amount of vegetation blocking our path. Although they were working on fixing it, if we ran into any problems, we shouldn't hesitate to ask for help. This news caused a slight change in my facial expression, but I remembered the philosophy of "c'est la vie" (such is life) and accepted that we would be the pioneers to cross this route after the period of inactivity.

Despite the language barrier, as I didn't speak French and the French weren't very proficient in English, we found a clever formula for communication. We quickly learned how to overcome any obstacles that arose during our journey, and the French were always ready to help us whenever we needed them. The adventure continued, and we were prepared to face any challenges that the river and nature had in store for us.

First border lock, France - Belgium. This is where you complete the procedures to obtain the pass, pay fees, receive information, and get the control to activate the locks.

Here, you can see this border lock. There are no markers leading to the river, so be cautious to avoid any distractions.

Full lock, France - Belgium border. This is a good place to ask for information about the canals, their condition, and water reservations, as they are

The Eastern Canal, a gem of French navigation, stretches like an interfluvial link connecting the majestic Meuse and the picturesque Moselle with the tranquil Saône. Its beginning lies in the charming town of Givet, located in the Ardennes department. Over a considerable stretch, it intertwines with the Marne-Rhine Canal in the Lorraine region, forming a journey of more than 20 kilometers before reaching its final destination in Corre, in the Haute-Saône department. This colossal canal, constructed between 1874 and 1887, spans a total of 439 kilometers.

Venturing into another country, and not just any country but one of great magnitude, it became evident that as we headed south, the workings of things became more bureaucratic and somewhat worn. However, this bureaucracy could not overshadow the undeniable beauty of this land. In my experience, I have crossed France in all directions on many occasions, and I can affirm that it is one of the best places in the world to live.

In this new stretch of our journey, we encountered locks that offered two operating options: some could be operated through a remote control, while others required entirely manual operation. The manual locks were divided into two distinct types, each with its specific purpose.

The first, marked with a blue bar, initiated the filling process. To set it in motion, we had to pull upward with force once everything was prepared and secured on the boat. This process was especially rewarding when we had the canal to ourselves. If there were other boats present, we coordinated the operation with the other navigators, and the lock was set in motion when everyone was ready.

The second bar with a red color was reserved for emergency situations. Activating it would trigger a siren that alerted the control center. The advantage was that the central base personnel would immediately respond in case of problems, rather than waiting for a local official to answer a phone call. We responded in English through a microphone to report that there hadn't been an accident, but rather the lock simply wasn't working, which alleviated the concerns of the workers.

Another of the manual locks had a peculiarity: a rope hung from a small crane, and as we passed underneath it, we had to grab the rope and pull it down. This operation had its fair share of humor because if you failed to hold onto the rope, you found yourself having to go back and make a second attempt. Without a doubt, this tested my agility to the limit and generated laughter on more than one occasion.

As we crossed into France, the topic of water took on an even more interesting dimension.

Our journey through the French canals proceeded calmly, always navigating in the center of the channel due to the frequent depth issues we encountered. Around us, fruit orchards, forests, and occasionally, impressive palaces and estates unfolded, creating a landscape of great beauty. As we progressed, the mountains and river bends became more frequent, which also meant more locks on our path.

In France, we faced stricter measures related to the COVID-19 pandemic, resulting in the closure of many places. However, we never lacked anything as we were in one of the most civilized regions in the world. One of the most common challenges we faced was the lack of places to moor if we didn't arrive in time to cross a lock. This posed a real problem, especially for us with our sailboat, as there was not enough space to dock. On numerous occasions, we were forced to backtrack several miles upstream in search of a suitable place to stop. This challenge became a highlight of our journey.

In the photo below, it was the last day with Felix. The lock closed, and there was no way to moor. It would have meant going back almost 6 miles, which didn't seem reasonable. Although it's prohibited, we secured a mooring under the gate. Besides being prohibited, it wasn't very pleasant to sleep there.

Here, we see the Colibrí with the bow wedged into the closed lock. We missed it by just 10 minutes. We moored at the bow, stern, and the starboard stern with a stake, and port stern to the lock. The lock never fully closed, causing a cascade at our stern. Many rocks on both sides.

You can also see the triangular traffic light used in France.

In the left image, it was the only lock that couldn't be activated either automatically or manually. The problem was the lack of water. Here, I had to wait for three hours for the water to accumulate and see if another boat would arrive to pass together, but no one came. You can also see the long ropes passed through the bollard. As the water level rises, one adjusts the ropes and balances the boat when the current rocks it.

In the right image, it was the lock that closed just as I showed in photos above, how we tied up like a spider. There was a red and green light that took 15 minutes to prepare, but at exactly 7 pm, another red light came on, and it went out of service.

On that afternoon, everything seemed tangled and filled with challenges. My companion Felix had to leave, and the situation was not favorable; there was only one bus passing by, and it was a Friday. So, I decided to accompany him to a nearby, quite isolated village. Felix's journey would be long and not without difficulties, as he had to use a respirator during the trip, which undoubtedly made it more complicated for him. But due to his unchangeable schedule, he had no other option but to depart.

Meanwhile, my plan was to get up an hour before the locks were opened. My goal was to cross to the other side and check if there was any boat coming in because, with the lock being full, the supposed boat on the other side would have priority. I should be prepared to get the sailboat out urgently. As you may have noticed, untying all those ropes without endangering the boat and avoiding a possible collision with the rocks represented one of the most challenging maneuvers of the entire journey.

First, I removed the two stern lines, and the sailboat became partially stable thanks to the current. Then the challenge was to release the two bow lines at the same time because any delay in either of them would cause the boat to tilt sharply to one side due to the current. There was no room for mistakes, and I knew that if I failed, the price would be high.

With the rudder pointing toward the lock, facing the current, I released the two bow lines and quickly moved to the stern to take control. When the boat tried to cross, I steered it towards the lock and then, at full reverse power, cut the throttle immediately to avoid a collision. It was a moment when I undoubtedly sweated a lot. I moved about 60 meters away, and after five minutes of tension, I was able to activate the gates with my remote control. It was an immense relief, and we continued our journey. At that moment, I realized that there are situations better avoided. The cost of an error in critical moments like that was too high. Sometimes, moving more slowly is the best option, and we should have gone back a few miles and moored the sailboat in a safer place.

After about 40 minutes, we were ready to continue on the other side of the lock. These locks, in general, raised our navigation level by about 2 to 4 meters. The geography had changed significantly here; the water was cleaner, with more vegetation and wildlife, making it clearer. The depth was consistent, around 1.7 or 1.8 meters, and the landscape was full of curves and mountains, a true wonder.

Sailing solo made the journey through the locks somewhat more complicated, but I knew that we set our own limits. It was a matter of being more cautious, placing more fenders, reducing speed, and making firm and determined moves as I approached the center of the lock, with no room for doubt. If something went wrong, I had a plan B: move the sailboat away from the wall, reverse, and start over.

When the sailboat remained motionless near the lock wall, I had approximately one minute before the turbulence pushed it backward or opened its bow inward into the lock. At that moment, I quickly grabbed the bow and stern ropes that I had previously prepared, placed them over my shoulder, and began to climb the ladder as high as possible. When I felt the four tons of the sailboat starting to move, I crossed the ropes quickly to the nearest bollard, secured them, and then returned to the sailboat. There, I climbed back up and adjusted the ropes, giving them a turn so that the rest of the rope returned to the sailboat. It's worth mentioning that it was prohibited to tie the ropes to the lock. Then, I descended quickly and remained alert throughout the filling operation.

Undoubtedly, the experience of navigating along this river journey had its unique challenges. During the first half of the journey, we encountered a constant ascent, facing upstream currents that challenged us at every step. Each time we entered the locks, the process involved gradually filling them, preparing for what would be a reverse operation during the descent. However, this phase, although different, turned out to be more manageable and promising, and I will provide a more detailed explanation later.

It's worth mentioning that the stairs we found inside the locks were always covered in mud, making them extremely slippery surfaces. In this challenging environment, we always moved with caution, secured with life jackets to ensure our safety at all times.

Once we crossed the locks, the canal narrowed significantly, pointing directly toward the imposing mountains. Initially, the geography of the valley seemed like a mystery, but as we traveled further inland, all doubts began to fade. In the distance, we spotted an entrance that left me astonished: a tunnel. The idea of taking a sailboat under the mountain was completely surreal and posed additional challenges, especially concerning the boat's draft. Now, we had to worry not only about the edges and walls but also about the tunnel's ceiling. The odyssey that awaited us became a moment of indescribable ecstasy, and even I couldn't believe what I was about to experience.

Upon entering the tunnel, a dim white light began to illuminate our path, which was a relief. Not only that, but it also helped our eyes adjust to the tunnel's dimness. With great caution and at a speed of approximately 2 knots, we advanced, aware of the walls around us and with the bow mostly out of our sight. However, what followed was a truly fabulous and challenging experience in equal measure. In total, we crossed three of these tunnels, one of which had an impressive diameter of 2 kilometers. It was truly mind-blowing, a feat that will be etched in our memory forever.

The first tunnel, what an adrenaline rush...

Canal de la Morne – au – Rhin.
Tunel de Foug - VNF

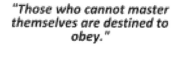

"Those who cannot master themselves are destined to obey."

Friedrich Nietzsche

Inside the tunnel, with our eyes accustomed to the surroundings, it was a lot of fun, a unique experience. If things were to take a bad turn, there was an escape route.

On the other side of the valley, navigation became a real challenge. Aquatic plants became our persistent enemies as they infiltrated the boat's cooling system, leaving us with the cumbersome task of stopping every few miles to reverse course and get rid of the stubborn plants entangled in the keel. Sometimes, these plants had so much power that they seemed to completely halt the progress of our sailboat, forcing us to go back and start the process again.

But the worst was yet to come. We encountered floating vines that seemed to have a singular purpose in life: entangling themselves in the propeller shaft. This not only put additional strain on the engine but sometimes required us to stop the boat completely and venture into the cold, mountain-fed water to untangle them. The water was notably cold, a constant reminder of the challenges we faced with my Colibrí, but there was no other choice. On several occasions, I encountered aquatic creatures, including large catfish that commanded respect and eels that stirred some unease. However, ultimately, I came to understand that the true predator in this environment was the human being, whose irresponsible actions often wreaked havoc on these delicate ecosystems.

Despite all these difficulties, these unexpected moments of plunging into the cold waters became a kind of mandatory bath, an experience that I faced with determination and, ultimately, even with enjoyment.

Another challenge we faced on this journey was the frequent early morning fog. This forced us to delay the start of our navigation since we knew we had a time limit before the locks closed. With each delay, the pressure increased, but we knew we had to face these challenges if we wanted to progress through this mountainous and unfamiliar landscape.

The operation of the locks was a delicate physical process that required a precise balance between water levels. For these gates to open, it was essential that more water entered than left. If algae obstructed the gates, we had to intervene ourselves if the maintenance staff was not available. They provided us with a special tool to remove the algae, and sometimes when the amount of algae was overwhelming, we had to wait for a barge to collect them. On two occasions, this led us to wait for hours, a reminder that time and patience were essential on this journey.

On one memorable occasion, we found ourselves in an unusual situation when four boats attempted to enter the same lock. This lock released more water than it received, which unbalanced the pressure and left us trapped there for five long hours.

In this evening, a good place to overnight, you can see a large mountain of trees. These are from the major storm that occurred months ago. They are very dangerous for navigation, but fortunately, we never encountered any

The officials seemed bewildered, and no one knew how to resolve the situation, or at least they were very good at disguising their lack of interest in solving the problem. However, my curiosity and my willingness to communicate despite language barriers led me to propose a solution. Through gestures, looks, and attitudes, I managed to explain the lock system to the officials.

Finally, I suggested that we use a car and a cable to pull the lock while I took the risk of entering the lock and placing a log approximately 40 cm wide between the two gates. I was aware that I was assuming all the responsibility for possible dangers, but the need to get out of that pressing situation was imperative. After burning a lot of clutch in the process, we managed to open the lock enough for me to jump inside and place the log. Eureka! Finally, more water began to enter than was flowing out behind, and after about 10 minutes, we managed to equalize the pressures and free ourselves.

On the left, a beautiful forest. Just five minutes earlier, I couldn't see 4 meters ahead due to the fog.

Below, a family of swans in the fog. The sounds in this setting were sublime.

Above, sailing on the Canal de l'Est. You can also see a yellow square in the photo; that was one of the controls for the locks.

On the left, gradually, the miles passed by. It's a beautiful canal.

The euphoria among the sailors and the officials was indescribable; we celebrated with jumps and hugs, as if we had won a game together. All that was missing was a barbecue and some beers to complete the sense of achievement, but instead, we proceeded to take the boats out of the lock and then tied them along the canal. There, we enjoyed some well-deserved beers as we spent the night, surrounded by the magical nocturnal sounds of the forest.

Here, you can see the VNF van pulling with a tied rope.

The Colibrí waiting to be released, with the other three boats behind it.

After so much work, here we had a few beers with our new travel companions. What else could we ask for!

At dawn the next day, I woke up with a strong hangover that made me reconsider my sailing plans. I longed for a more relaxed day on the water, and as if destiny had planned it, I started encountering picturesque towns along my route. What surprised me the most was the large number of bohemians, writers, and other free spirits who had made their boats their homes. The beauty of this lifestyle immediately captivated me, and I found myself imagining what it would be like to lead such an existence.

The people I met in these floating towns exuded joy, kindness, and a deep sense of peace. I couldn't help but rub my eyes more than once, as if to make sure I wasn't dreaming. Every corner seemed to be imbued with a magical atmosphere that made you forget the worries of the outside world.

In case my journey became impossible due to water depth or any other circumstances, I had made an important decision: to return to these charming places and stay there until the seasonal rains made the waters navigable again. I was sure that if that happened, I would learn some French during my stay here. After all, any experience would be enriching in this unique environment.

However, for now, my destiny did not lead me in that direction.

In the picture above, we crossed a beautiful village. It was one of the oldest canals in France. Along this same canal, you can go to Switzerland and Germany from Belgium. The Meuse canal passes through Charleville-Mézières, Sedan, Verdun, Nancy, Épinal, and Mulhouse, rejoining the Rhine River. From there, where these rivers ended, was where our story with the Colibrí began.

Ancient cargo boats restored as homes.

Upon waking up the next morning, I followed my instincts and tracked the delightful aroma of fresh bread to a local bakery in the area. After enjoying a comforting breakfast, I continued my journey and, to my surprise, discovered a campsite that offered affordable moorings, around six euros per night. The atmosphere at the campsite was exceptional: there was a friendly community, and the facilities included quality showers. I decided it was the perfect place to take a few days of rest, give my sailboat a good wash, and carry out the necessary maintenance tasks.

Over time, I realized that I was no longer filling my water and gasoline tanks to 100 percent. Every centimeter of draft was valuable, and my boat began to have less margin in that regard. Until that moment, I had never experienced my boat's keel touching the riverbed. Of course, I had some encounters with the river bottom in the past, but they were generally abrupt stops that didn't cause significant damage and were easily overcome. However, while navigating through a narrow canal, my boat hit a submerged tree root on one occasion, and that sensation was like hitting a speed bump in the middle of the road. I must admit that it hurt me both physically and in my soul.

Under the influence of an optimistic mood and the prospect of exceptionally good weather, I made the decision to continue my journey. The sun was shining brightly, indicating that the water would gradually evaporate over the coming days, so there was no reason to stop.

The area I was sailing through was truly beautiful. The canals meander through curves, and on both sides, there were fields of fruit trees, corn, hemp, and other crops. On more than one occasion, I allowed myself the indulgence of mooring my boat and enjoying a fresh peach or some plums, or even picking some ears of corn. There was nothing like tasting something so fresh and delicious directly from the source, although I always made sure not to overindulge in my small harvest.

In these canals, there were rarely buoys or navigation marks, unlike the rivers where there was more frequent but still limited signage. At times, the rivers would widen and open into expansive lagoons, creating breathtaking bodies of water that left me breathless. Around noon, with my stomach starting to growl, and after making good progress, I came across a lagoon approximately one kilometer long by 600 meters wide. The sun was at its peak, and the lagoon was teeming with wildlife; it was like a dream come true. At that moment, I decided to venture into the lagoon and, later on, let my boat drift as I prepared a delicious meal. It was an absolute delight.

However, my happiness was abruptly interrupted when, about 100 meters into the lagoon and sailing at around 3.5 knots, my keel hit something with a shocking force. I had never experienced anything like it before. I was sure it wasn't a rock. My heart was racing as I shut off the engine and activated the emergency protocol to check for any signs of a water leak. I hurried to find wooden plugs and more equipment and made my way to the bilge. It was incredible; my sailboat was barely moving, but I could feel the water's movement beneath me. I was stranded but not on solid ground.

After inspecting the bilges, the inside of the hull, and the keel's shaft, I didn't find any obvious damage. I kept the VHF radio on hand, ready to send a distress signal if the boat started sinking, but luckily, that didn't happen. When I finally went outside, I could see that I had collided with a decaying tree. It was likely that the area was flooded, but I was to blame for this situation for leaving the marked channel.

It was clear that I needed to get out of there and return to the channel. I moored the sailboat with stakes and proceeded to release 150 liters of ballast water. With considerable effort and the engine at full power, my sailboat finally moved slowly and broke free from its entrapment on the tree. It was a tremendous relief.

From that moment on, I promised myself that I would never again leave the marked areas. I had made a human error, and I was determined to learn from it. I had full confidence in my sailboat, the Colibri from the Van De Stadt shipyard. It was a sturdy vessel with impeccable marine design, built with great attention to quality and durability.

At dawn the next day, while waiting patiently for the traffic lights to activate, I faced a peculiar maneuver that I had already mastered in my journey: approaching the traffic light with the sailboat at minimum speed and pulling a specific rope that activated the traffic light, indicating the right of way based on the side executed. This system was essential in this stretch of the journey and required precise execution.

Once inside the tunnel, I experienced a wonderful sensation that I had felt on previous occasions. However, upon exiting the tunnel, I noticed a significant slowdown, and I realized that the bow of my sailboat was covered with more algae than in any other part of the journey. I knew that if the boat came to a complete stop, it would be stranded in an unfavorable location because the exit of a tunnel was not the best place to face that situation. Quickly, I increased the engine's power to 3600 RPM, and the Colibri responded, but the algae remained attached to the hull.

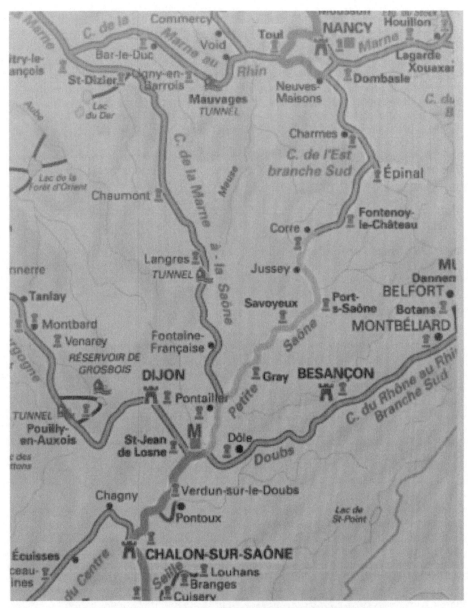

New navigation map, now through the center of France.

Fortunately, I managed to reach a sandy area free of algae but filled with a significant accumulation of plant debris. I decided to stop there to deal with the situation.

The scene before me was entirely wild, except for the large engineering works that reminded me of human presence. There was no sign of human life in sight, only lush nature surrounding my sailboat, which was now completely immobilized by the thick tangle of plants and algae that had built up on its hull.

With no other option, I had to dive under the boat. It was very early in the day, and the sun's rays were barely peering over the horizon, which meant the water was extremely cold. However, there was no alternative. Equipped with a knife attached to a line to prevent it from sinking to the bottom, a snorkel, and a swimsuit, I plunged into the icy waters. It had been a long time since I had felt such intense cold, but in situations like these, there's no room for doubt.

With each stroke, I delved into the tangle of plants and algae, carefully removing the vegetation that had clung to the hull of my sailboat. My main goal was to reach the daggerboard and clean the propeller and motor shaft. However, the cold was getting more intense with each minute underwater, and I couldn't bear it any longer. I emerged, semi-frozen, and finished the task from the boat's deck, soaked but determined.

It was an unforgettable moment, an enriching experience that reminded me of the importance of perseverance in the face of adversity. After completing the task, I enjoyed a comforting cup of hot coffee that helped me warm up. It was a reminder that even in the most challenging moments, valuable lessons can be found, and a little comfort can make it all worthwhile.

I decided to move forward, navigating the first 30 meters of clear water until I encountered another dense jungle of algae that extended for 50 meters. However, my destination was the next lock's quay, and I was determined to reach it without letting anything stop me. I accelerated at full speed, feeling how I gradually slowed down as I approached my goal.

Finally, I reached the desired spot and proceeded to clean everything necessary before waiting there. In that lock, which was part of a system of six cascading locks, I found that the first one was inactive. I immediately contacted the control center to report the situation, and after half an hour of uncertainty, someone showed up. It seemed that the operator had fallen asleep and inadvertently triggered a series of events. His demeanor was not friendly at all.

I inquired about the navigation in that section, and I was surprised when the official told me that my sailboat couldn't continue due to the lack of water. He suggested I should turn back, an idea that left me bewildered. As I contemplated this suggestion, examining the navigational charts, I realized that going back would entail an additional ten-day detour, going upstream on the River Rhine, which had its own difficulties. Additionally, I remembered the dense algae I had encountered along the way, which made the idea of turning back seem impractical.

I returned to the official's cabin and explained the whole situation, but his indifferent attitude persisted. Finally, I made the decision to continue, even if it meant facing potentially shallower canals that could trap me. It was a tough decision, but I executed it with determination.

The official activated the locks, and I continued my journey. Six locks further down, I reached the main VNF offices, where I decided to take a break and enjoy a good cup of coffee. There, by chance, I met the head of the section, an extremely friendly man fascinated by the stories of sailors like me. When I told him about my experience with the lack of water, he took me to his office and contacted each of the six or seven locks in question. They all confirmed that my sailboat had the necessary draft, and they had no knowledge of who had given incorrect information.

At that moment, I concluded that the previous official had tried to sabotage my journey with malicious lies. In front of his boss, I submitted a written complaint detailing all the events that had occurred, hoping that this person would face the consequences of their actions. It is unfortunate to encounter such dishonest individuals on the way.

Despite the adversities, by the end of this experience, I had the feeling that karma was on my side, and I decided to leave behind what had happened.

Our immediate destination was Épinal, from where we would begin to ascend the final kilometers of our journey to the highest point, at an altitude of 346 meters. This section was surrounded by majestic mountains and featured a narrow and shallow canal that, at times, lacked sufficient water. Before embarking on this challenge, I knew I had to inquire in Épinal about the navigational conditions in that stretch. If the waters were too low, I would have to consider an alternative route through the Rhine River, crossing Switzerland and descending through the south of that country since the Rhine maintained its flow throughout the year.

While continuing my journey, I noticed a hanging line with a crane to my starboard side, and I understood that this was another way to activate passage, in this case through a tunnel. Entry into the tunnel was not permitted until a clear green light was displayed. If another boat was already passing through, the situation became complicated. Since it was late, and I had found a good floating quay, I decided to spend the night there.

The environment was truly beautiful, tranquil, and safe. However, the night was not as peaceful as expected, as nature seemed to come to life in every corner. I even heard the howling of wolves in the distance. It was a wonder to gaze at the starry sky from the deck of the sailboat in the middle of the night, with nature reclaiming its space in this region. Moments like these made life worthwhile, and I hoped to experience many more of them.

Unfortunately, I don't have photographs of my ascent through the Épinal locks, but let me describe the physical experience I went through, which was truly exhausting. In a single day, I crossed a total of fourteen locks, each with its filling and activation times. This task requires exceptional physical fitness, and I'm not sure if I had it at that time. My hands ended up in a terrible state after manipulating the gates and ropes (cavos), and despite all my efforts, I barely advanced five miles in the entire day. Additionally, as I gained altitude, the nights became extremely cold, and the mornings brought dense fog that made navigation impossible.

In this region, I must admit that the canals were better maintained, and there were fewer algae compared to previous sections. Upon reaching the highest point of the journey, I knew that we would cross to another valley and begin the descent. This moment marked the halfway point of my journey, and although I felt joy for what I had achieved so far, I also experienced a deep sense of nostalgia for what I had left behind.

One detail I didn't mention earlier is that when crossing each region, it was necessary to obtain a new control to activate the locks. They don't automatically provide you with a new control; you have to visit the local office and request it. The system doesn't seek you out automatically, so you need to be attentive to this process.

However, one of the most astonishing surprises I experienced during my journey was when, in the midst of my exhausting routine, I noticed the canal losing its vegetation on its sides. By paying closer attention, I realized that I was facing a large aqueduct that crossed over a river. It was a surreal experience to see the river flowing beneath the canal, a true marvel that highlighted the diversity of landscapes I encountered on my voyage.

"Everything can be taken from a man but one thing: the last of the human freedoms—to choose one's attitude in any given set of circumstances."

Viktor Frankl

After a few well-deserved days of rest and facing a steep ascent from Espinal, I finally reached the highest point of my journey, approximately 346 meters above sea level. The feeling of reaching this peak was overwhelming, and I knew I was about to enter a different stage of my river adventure.

The landscape transformed as I progressed. The canals grew wider, and dense forests surrounded me, creating an atmosphere of tranquility and mystery. Surprisingly, the locks were now less frequent, marking a change in the river's topography. It was then that I realized I had reached the waters of the Petit Saone, the precursor to the Saone River, which would later join other tributaries to form the majestic Rhone, a river that would take me towards the Mediterranean on an exciting river journey.

The Saone River is a natural wonder in eastern France, known as the main tributary of the Rhone that feeds it from the north.

His numbers are impressive: a length of 480 kilometers and an extensive basin of 29,950 square kilometers. But what truly makes it special is its connection to the geography and life in the region. The Doubs River, its main tributary, significantly contributes to its flow and ecological importance.

Despite my initial concerns about the draft, the Petit Saone pleasantly surprised me. The canals were in excellent condition, and the locks were filled with water, indicating that it was time to start descending. This new direction of water flow, along with a slight downstream current, translated to less diesel consumption and more efficient progress.

As I sailed down the Petit Saone, I noticed that life on the river was becoming more vibrant. Barges and houseboats became more frequent, making me feel like I was entering an area conducive to an extended stay. Although these vessels had shallow drafts, requiring caution when navigating, the picturesque and tranquil surroundings were tempting.

However, my exciting journey came to an abrupt halt when, near lock 15 after passing Espinal, I experienced a sudden stop. My sailboat became immobilized, and I was certain that the keel had become embedded in the riverbed mud. This situation was challenging and left me bewildered, unsure of how to proceed.

My initial reaction was to throw a line from the stern to a cleat on the canal's edge. Then, despite the accumulated mud, I ventured into the water. Swimming to the wooden and brass edge of the canal was far from pleasant, but I did it carefully and determinedly.

Once on solid ground, I exerted all my strength to pull the line, using a nearby tree as a point of leverage, but the keel remained unmoved, and the slight current did not help at all. I spent about an hour in this situation while mentally exploring my options. It was at that moment when two Dutch cyclists passing by the area offered their help in a supportive manner. The three of us stood there, contemplating together how to resolve this unexpected challenge.

Finally, a clever idea came to me. With six hands available, I decided to tie a line to the mid-mast of my sailboat. The cyclists could then tilt the vessel while I used the engine in an effort to free the stuck keel. I didn't hesitate and returned to the water, still covered in mud but determined to put an end to this complication.

Implementing this strategy, I noticed the keel slowly beginning to give way.

With my new companions on land pulling the line and tilting the sailboat while I increased the engine to 3600 RPM, we finally managed to free the vessel. It was an exciting and relieving moment, and the cyclists released the line before following me on their bikes as I continued through the remaining muddy meters without losing power. Finally, I arrived at the next lock, where the draft was sufficient to continue my thrilling journey.

This episode served as a reminder of the unpredictability and beauty of exploring the rivers and canals of France. Each day brought new experiences and challenges, but also the opportunity to meet generous and supportive people who crossed my path, making every moment of this river journey truly unforgettable.

My journey continued full of challenges and surprises, and this time, both I and my companion, the hummingbird, faced an unforgettable experience. I had managed to activate the lock precisely at 7:00 PM, but suddenly, everything came to a sudden halt. Night had fallen, and it was no longer the right time for navigation; the system was out of service. Although I knew it was strictly forbidden to remain inside a lock overnight, I decided to take that risk without knowing the possible consequences that awaited me.

The hours passed, and in the darkness, around 3:30 in the morning, I began to hear voices and see flashlights approaching. Someone knocked on the hull of my boat, getting my attention. When I emerged, I encountered two men who seemed somewhat irritated. I explained my situation and how I had become trapped inside the lock, choosing to spend the night there rather than risking running aground again while removing my sailboat. To my relief, the two employees showed understanding and empathy. They worked diligently to assist me in any way they could.

However, the urgency was evident: my sailboat had to be removed from the lock immediately. The main issue was that the lock gate had been improperly closed, resulting in a significant loss of water. This situation severely affected eight locks in the area, all of which had insufficient draft for navigation. I realized that, unwittingly, I had caused quite a mess that needed to be resolved without delay.

The following morning presented an additional challenge. I couldn't resume my journey until well into the afternoon, as it took many hours for the locks to recover. Fortunately, time and the current managed to resolve the situation. In hindsight, I realized how lucky I had been in the midst of this complicated situation.

From that moment on, I enjoyed some of the most relaxed days of the entire journey. I decided to limit my navigation to five hours a day and make the most of the remaining time to enjoy a true vacation within the vacation. These moments were precious and well-deserved. Walks through the surrounding forests, reading, cooking, and performing maintenance tasks on my boat became the leisurely rhythm of my days. With my faithful companion, the Hummingbird, by my side, we savored this break as we continued our descent down the river, ready for whatever the next stage of the journey had in store for us.

An experience I will never forget happened at lock 17, a place that had a somewhat eerie and abandoned atmosphere. Once, this site was inhabited by someone responsible for the process and maintenance, but at that moment, everything operated automatically, and there was no one in sight. As is well known, one of the key pieces of advice when dealing with locks is to maintain a safe distance when they are activated. During the filling and emptying of locks, there is usually significant turbulence, and it is recommended to stay at a minimum distance of 30 to 40 meters. However, on this occasion, I grew complacent and perhaps ventured too close.

I stayed here for two days. The water was crystal clear, teeming with aquatic life, both animal and plant. I enjoyed many snorkeling sessions, a lot of reading, and finally, the quiet surroundings and the passage of time signaled that I could continue my journey...

When the activation process began, I was only 10 meters away from the gate, with the engine idling, patiently waiting for the traffic light to turn green. But what happened next was a reminder of how unpredictable river navigation can be. The gates opened, and water was still rushing in, creating significant whirlpools. In a matter of seconds, my sailboat started to spin towards the gate, with the bow pointing directly at a rock pillar.

It was a distressing moment, but I acted on instinct. I grabbed one of the boat's fenders and ran to the bow, arriving just seconds before the impending disaster. I positioned the fender and averted the collision. Then, with a pounding heart, I quickly returned to the cabin and tried to move forward, but the sailboat was already crosswise, just one meter away from impact. Fortunately, the water pressure equalized, stopping the vessel, but I couldn't prevent a significant impact on the stern. Although the hull fiberglass was resilient and there were no leaks, the mark on the boat would be a constant reminder of lock 17.

After spending a night at the location, filled with disappointment for not handling the situation more effectively, I decided to take a breather. Three locks downstream, I paused my journey, prepared a delicious meal, and opened a bottle of fine red wine. Often, when facing tough times, we can get stuck in resentment. However, I believe that if you truly learn something valuable from those situations, you can become a better person.

That night was a unique experience, as I had never before heard so many wolves so close. Their howls echoed through the air, instilling a sense of respect for nature. I was in their territory, without any risks but also without civilization in sight, making it even more awe-inspiring. During those 12 hours, I could reflect, rest, and learn.

The next day, despite not having slept very well, I continued my journey with a renewed sense of determination and respect for nature. It was a reminder of the unpredictability and beauty of life on the water, a lesson I would carry with me in every stage of my journey.

As I continued my descent down the river, it was enriched by the confluence of numerous smaller tributaries. Suddenly, I found myself navigating much wider and more voluminous waters, free from the concerns of draft and the counter-currents I had experienced before. The feeling was that of everything moving with renewed speed, and while I was on a larger river, I also noticed the presence of floating logs along my route, a reminder of the force of nature in these waters.

The lock 17 building had a different appearance at night.

River traffic began to gradually increase, and the locks I encountered along my path became more impressive and majestic. During this stretch, I had been in contact with my uncle Luis, who resided in Barcelona and shared my adventurous spirit. He was eager to join me on this journey, and we had planned to meet a few days later.

On a particular afternoon, as I crossed the city of Chalon-sur-Saône, I spotted a suitable place to moor my considerably draft vessel. I decided it was the right place to spend the rest of the day, taking the opportunity to explore the city, recharge, and continue my journey early in the morning.

However, the tranquility of the night was suddenly disrupted around 1:30 in the morning. A thunderous boat horn sound jolted me out of bed. Stepping outside, I was faced with a challenging situation: a tourist ferry had arrived without prior notice, and I was not exactly in its way, but in the path of its maneuver. The ferry's crew was visibly upset and urged me to leave the area immediately or face possible penalties. Without delay, I started the engine and prepared my boat to depart within minutes, thus avoiding any unpleasant consequences.

At that crucial moment, I realized that I was about to embark on my first night navigation on a river. Honestly, it was not something I would recommend or find enjoyable. Navigating solely relying on a 100% plotter on a river was no joke. However, the positive aspect of the situation was that the river stretch I was navigating was well marked with buoys.

I remembered that, generally, where there are locks, there are also waiting docks. I had about 5 miles of downstream navigation ahead, and there weren't many alternatives. As I approached, I recall how I followed the powerful lock lights, knowing that this would be one of the most uncomfortable navigations I had experienced in a long time.

When I finally arrived at the dock below the lock, I moored the sailboat and watched as the large French locks continued to operate even at night. I decided it would be wiser to wait until dawn to pass through them.

As I prepared to settle in and get some rest, I noticed a large boat approaching. My sailboat was about 300 meters from the lock, on the dock. As the massive cruise ship slowed down, it generated a small but powerful wave. I remember rushing out and watching my sailboat, the "Colibri," start to move towards the river due to the force of the wave, breaking the stern line in the process.

A river cruise ship similar to the one that broke my stern line passed through this point later on.

The wall at the far end was where I had entered, estimating about 14 meters in total; we were not quite there yet...

There was no time to think; I just acted on instinct. I grabbed the boat hook (a pole with a hook, for those who may not know) and jumped from the boat to the dock. I'm not sure how I did it, but I managed to catch the sailboat and drag the stern back to its original position, securing it with a thicker line. It was a terrifying experience, and it was clear that I wouldn't be able to sleep that night.

One of the best decisions I made before embarking on this adventure was to make sure I had plenty of fenders, some larger than necessary for my boat. But that night, those fenders turned out to be an unexpected salvation in the midst of a distressing situation.

The next day, when I woke up, I felt noticeably tired and eagerly wanted to put some distance between myself and the place where I had spent an uncomfortable night. I prepared the boat carefully and patiently, aware that I needed to be in good shape for the next leg of my journey. As I waited patiently for about 30 minutes for the large lock to fill, I reflected on the peculiarity of the situation.

Entering that enormous lock, being the only boat present, was a somewhat surreal experience. It was astonishing to think of the tons of water that were being moved just to accommodate a small boat like mine. However, in this part of the world, water was not a scarce resource, and that was the established operation.

The image of my boat inside the immense lock, surrounded by concrete walls and the sound of water filling the space, left a lasting impression in my mind. I was ready to continue my journey, knowing that each day on the river brought new adventures and unique experiences.

In these latitudes, the river already carries a considerable amount of water, making navigation very comfortable. Sometimes, I even enjoy a favorable current, reaching speeds of up to 2 knots, perfect for relaxing and admiring the beautiful landscape around me. This area of the river is dotted with major cities, and every time I pass through one of them, I am amazed by their architecture, majestic bridges, and the bustling urban life. I also always take advantage of these stops to look for gas stations and refuel.

However, refueling in this region is not a simple task, as I mentioned at the beginning. It's essential to have a trolley to transport the load without risking your back. River traffic in this area is quite intense, so you must be vigilant at all times. One of the most complicated situations is when we enter the locks and the large commercial vessels do not turn off their engines. Instead, they simply secure the bow and keep the engine running while pressing against the lock wall. This maneuver creates turbulent currents that can be dangerous for sailboats and small boats.

One of the most challenging situations we face when entering locks is how large commercial vessels handle their engines. Instead of shutting them off, these maritime giants simply secure their bow and use the power of their engines to press against the lock wall. As you can imagine, this generates unpredictable currents that can be extremely dangerous for sailboats and smaller vessels.

My unwavering advice is to maintain a safe distance from this maneuver whenever possible. If you have the option, approaching the bow of the commercial ship is preferable, although in some cases, circumstances may not allow for much choice in this matter. I've witnessed situations where authorities were forced to remove smaller vessels from the lock to make way for an approaching large passenger ship.

The French countryside, places like these, you have to keep an eye on the depth sounder.

Saône River, urban landscape in Lyon.

It is crucial to understand that non-compliance with these rules can have serious consequences and delay the entire process of transiting through the lock. Therefore, it is essential to follow the instructions and remain alert at all times to ensure safe and incident-free navigation in these unique river traffic conditions.

As we move towards the end of the Saône River, the landscapes change, adopting a more rural and tranquil character. The river's waters become more serene, and the large locks of France begin to appear on the horizon, marking a new stage in our journey.

Crossing the Pierre-Bénite lock, an incredible wind Venturi is created, along with passing a substantial waterfall of water. There, you see the green light, and we are authorized to proceed.

The city of Lyon, with its magnificence and cosmopolitan diversity, is an iconic place where two rivers of great significance converge: the Saône and the famous Rhône. These rivers, although mostly substantial in flow, used to face draft issues during drought periods in this region. In response to this situation, significant measures were taken to ensure the navigation of large vessels.

It was in Lyon where the largest lock in all of France and our journey, the Pierre-Bénite Lock, was erected. This imposing engineering feat is simply impressive. From the moment you enter it, you can feel goosebumps, and if there are other boats sharing the lock, the tension in the air is palpable. As smaller boaters, we must always enter last and secure ourselves quickly, as the closing process is activated once the lock gate line is crossed.

At this stage of my experience, I have accumulated a great deal of knowledge and skills to tackle these situations. Although each lock is unique, the techniques we employ are often similar, allowing us to approach these complex maneuvers with confidence and precision. Each journey is an opportunity to learn and hone our skills, making every day on the water a new adventure filled with exciting challenges.

This is an example of a bollard inside the lock, where we pass lines without tying them. In this case, the wall is so large that beneath the bollard, there is a large airtight tank that raises and lowers the bollard. Well thought out!

On the left, our makeshift cover on the stern of the Colibrí, and in the background, you can see where we had entered just minutes before...

Pierre-Bénite lock, red light, we have to hold our position. The mud mark on the wall indicates how much we are descending.

The Rhône, one of the most significant rivers in Central Europe, represents the main artery of the Mediterranean region, crossing Switzerland and France. With an impressive length of 812 kilometers, this river feeds a vast basin of 97,800 square kilometers, the majority of which is in France.

As we exited the majestic Pierre-Bénite lock, we were venturing into the last great river before reaching the vast Mediterranean. This odyssey became even more memorable as my uncle, an experienced sailor who had sailed the waters of the Mediterranean in his catamaran in the past, joined the journey. Welcome, Luis!

At this stage of the journey, memories are filled with great storms and alerts about the rising river flow. Despite having the current in our favor and a sufficient draft, I didn't see a reason to be concerned until I was warned about the amount of logs and debris the river tended to carry. This completely changed the situation and led me to the decision to seek refuge in a nearby port.

After sailing a few more miles, I found a port and a friendly sailor who came over in his zodiac to receive me and guide me to where I would moor my boat. When I mentioned my draft, he didn't seem to worry, which made me think everything would be fine. However, about 15 meters from the spot, my sailboat, the "Colibrí," settled into the mud as if it were a finger sinking into a mud pie.

Fortunately, I was protected from the river's current, but with the risk of rising water levels, my sailboat could drift without being secured. I managed to free the boat by reversing toward the stern, but when I tried to enter the main channel of the port, my sailboat ran aground again. At that moment, the sailor didn't know how to help me and, as mysteriously as he appeared, he left. His lack of assistance didn't concern me too much, as I was determined to resolve the situation on my own.

Finally, I noticed that there was a fueling platform when entering the river. Although sleeping there was prohibited, I considered it the best option in this exceptional situation. None of us smoked, and we planned to eat out, so we decided to spend the night there. Undoubtedly, it was the right choice at that moment.

One of the most beautiful aspects of any adventure is how unexpected challenges become opportunities to demonstrate our ability to overcome obstacles and keep moving forward. In my case, I see every problem as a valuable lesson, and since there is always something new to learn, I consider everything positive.

"An intelligent person can sit on an anthill, but only a fool remains sitting on it."

Chinese Proverb

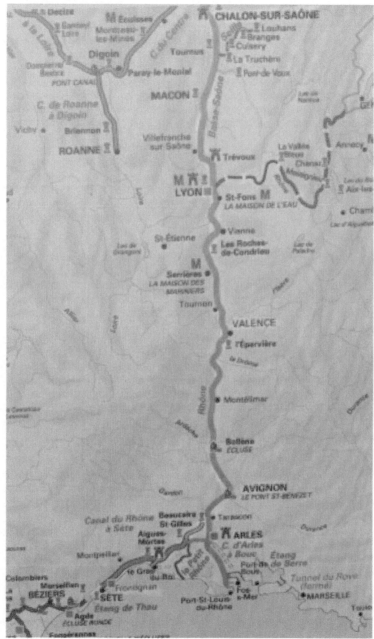

New navigation map, Rhône River

Rhône River, Luis grabbing the famous boat hook, very important throughout the journey.

Restaurants on very old towboats, all restored, very picturesque along the Rhône.

Even though the river had slightly increased its water level, it was nothing out of the ordinary and didn't carry any plant debris. I knew that in a few hours, my guest sailor would approach, which encouraged me to open a bottle of excellent red wine and enjoy a meal right there. These little moments are the soul of life, and as I looked towards the horizon, I saw another brave adventurer approaching. How wonderful life is!

This stretch of the journey passed quickly, with the constant 2-knot current in our favor and the limited number of locks, allowing us to maintain an excellent pace. However, the time we had budgeted for this stage of the trip was rapidly running out, and we had only one week left. Our next goal was to reach Arles and from there divert towards Sète through the canals, following the course of the Petit-Rhône.

During this part of the river, we encountered numerous sailboats that were also descending towards the Mediterranean. Some of them were only traveling the river, which made the navigation even more enriching.

In the image, we can appreciate the enormous size of this lock, all that we have descended, seeing the mud on the wall. Also, the other large ship that generates turbulence with its engines, and most importantly, I wanted to show you that in each rectangular opening towards the top, there are these floating bollards (noray), which are impossible to use in small boats, so you have to use crossing lines from the bow to the stern. When you see the bow or stern rise, you pull the opposite one, and that's how you can empty the lock in this case.

Castle on the banks of the Rhône River, in the past, everything revolved around rivers, which is why throughout the journey, I have seen incredible and inhospitable medieval architectures. France has many of these well-kept secrets.

At night, we would gather at the mooring areas. It was evident that we were the sailors who had come from the farthest away, as our courtesy flags revealed our origins.

In this region, there are plenty of marinas and boat campgrounds. The access costs are usually symbolic, and in return, they provide services like electricity, water, and bathrooms. After a long day of sailing, there was nothing more comforting than enjoying a good hot shower. On board the "Colibri," we had a 12V portable shower that we would often place a 30-liter water container on deck to warm up a bit. However, in this stretch of the river, we didn't use it as frequently.

Throughout the entire journey, we noticed that there weren't many fueling stations for boats. That's why carrying jerry cans and a cart to transport them became an essential strategy to ensure we had enough fuel at each stage of the crossing. This meticulous planning allowed us to maintain our independence and enjoy the journey without worries.

As we made our way toward the Mediterranean, with all the experience we had accumulated on our journey, navigation not only became less complicated but also much faster. The process of crossing the locks was highly automated at this stage of the trip, and while it took away some of the charm of the smaller locks we had passed through weeks earlier, it was a testament to the evolution of navigation along our route. So far, we had crossed more than 180 locks, and my hands proudly displayed the marks of a true sailor.

The climate in this part of the valley had undergone a noticeable change, marking the transition to the Mediterranean climate. We had to be very mindful of the famous tramontana, as the strong gusts of wind were far from pleasant when you were in a narrow canal surrounded by rocks.

A few miles before reaching Arles, we faced a somewhat peculiar maneuver. After passing through a lock, we had to navigate a few meters upstream and then return about 200 meters downstream to enter the Petit Rhône canal. This canal, with a moderate flow and no significant currents, ran parallel to the Mediterranean Sea in the direction of Sète. Although we had the option to head directly out to the sea from Arles, we considered it more romantic to continue along the canals. Besides, I had planned to raise the mast in Sète or Agde, which would add a special touch to our journey.

The Petit Rhône, also known as the Little Rhône, originates from the main course of the Grand Rhône, north of the city of Arles. From this point, the Petit Rhône heads west, while the main river continues its course southeastward. This divergence creates the largest river delta in Europe, an area of great geographical and ecological importance.

Finally, the Petit Rhône majestically flows into the Mediterranean Sea, completing its journey from the high mountains to the ocean.

A key element in navigating this region is the Saint-Gilles Canal, which connects to the Rhône to Sète Canal. This waterway allows effective communication with the city of Sète and offers the opportunity to continue the journey along the Canal du Midi and the Canal du Garonne, eventually reaching the Atlantic Ocean. While the Saint-Gilles Canal does not play a significant economic role, it has become a vital resource for sports and recreational navigation and provides access for boaters to the homes along its banks. The region is a paradise for those who enjoy recreational boating and seek the tranquility and beauty of the surroundings.

As we ventured into these canals, we experienced a change in pace and atmosphere that induced a sense of calm. Since they are entirely automated, there is no strict control over the validity of passes, adding a touch of relaxation to the experience.

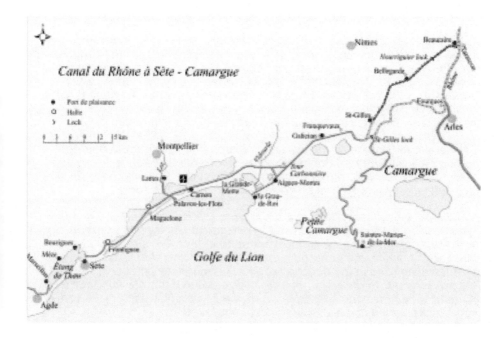

The waters in this region are known for their high salinity and characteristic turbidity, which surprisingly contributes to the flourishing of wildlife. In fact, we are in the heart of Europe's great delta, a paradise for fauna.

In this environment, the diversity of bird species is impressive, and among them, the flamingo stands out for its incomparable beauty. Their feathers take on a vibrant pink hue due to the pigments in their diet, creating a truly dazzling sight. It's a wonderful spectacle to observe these majestic birds in their natural habitat, adding a touch of color to the tranquil serenity of the canals.

However, we also noticed an interesting aspect of regulation in this area. Given the absence of significant commercial traffic, some companies allow anyone to rent large boats without requiring any kind of study or license. This, in turn, has led to uncomfortable and dangerous situations for navigation. The lack of restrictions can be a double-edged sword, as it provides freedom to boaters but also presents challenges in terms of safety and control in these waters.

In light of the situation, we decided to apply the golden rule of navigation: maintain a safe distance and be cautious. We had witnessed various incidents and accidents that left us perplexed due to the lack of experience of some boaters.

With the forecast of an increase in the strength of the tramontana in the coming days, we decided to take precautions before the storm arrived. We searched for a suitable place to moor our boat and wait there for the weather to develop, for as long as necessary. Finally, we found a small fishing village with a sturdy seawall that seemed like the perfect place to observe the storm's impact on the canals.

This picturesque village used to be a haven of tranquility, but unfortunately, the invasion of tourists on rental boats had transformed the serenity into a hubbub. We learned through weather apps that winds of up to 24 knots with gusts reaching 28-30 knots were expected. It's important to remember that in these narrow canals, where the margins are tight, such weather conditions can be challenging.

As the hours passed, the typical clouds of strong winds began to gather on the horizon, and as if on cue, an initial gust made its entrance. I was on the deck with a cup of coffee in hand, prepared to witness the spectacle. Tourists on other boats were nervous, and some of them seemed to be causing more trouble than necessary. Now, as I write what I witnessed, I realize that maybe I should have distanced myself from that tumult of amateur sailors.

At that critical moment, at least five boats of about 10 meters in length and 4 meters in width began colliding with each other and with the edges of the canals. These boats, with a high freeboard and shallow draft, collided chaotically. In the midst of this confusion, an inexperienced boater tried to moor his boat near mine, and that's when all my alarms went off. I yelled at him to get away, but the man seemed completely out of control at the helm. I changed my tone and, aware that I was speaking to someone who had completely lost control of the situation, offered to help if he threw two lines to secure himself. However, a powerful gust of wind caused his boat to head directly toward mine, with the power of his engines adding even more chaos to the scene. I rushed to the bow of my boat and placed the largest fenders available. Then, as I headed to the stern, knowing I wouldn't make it in time, I threw a fender, but unfortunately, it didn't land in the right position. The sound of the impact was deafening; they had struck the portside hull of my vessel. Frustration and anger overwhelmed me, knowing that all of this could have been avoided.

At that moment, I firmly told him that he must immediately remove his boat. I threatened to board his vessel and take control if he didn't move away, and upon hearing these words and seeing the damage done, the man finally started his engine and withdrew, hitting other boats in his path. It was a moment of great stress and anger.

However, as I mentioned earlier, in the tough moments of life, it's important to find positive aspects to grow as individuals.

First bridge, entrance to Sète, France.

Downtown Sète, very beautiful, as you can see, not every canal is navigable by every vessel, and we couldn't pass through this one.

In the midst of this stressful situation, I started to think positively. The fact that my vessel had been damaged in the same place where it had suffered an accident in the lock a few days earlier meant that the insurance should cover all the necessary repairs. With that last sip of coffee, I prepared to track down the reckless captain; he had to take responsibility and pay for the damages he had caused.

Arriving in Frontignan a few miles from Sète, there is a fork in the canal that allows you to either go through the towns or head out to the sea. Our plan was to go out to the sea and make our way to the port of Sète, but in this canal, where they were dredging, the depth sounder basically went crazy, beeping incessantly. We had to stop the engine and turn back the way we came. We still couldn't navigate the sea, so we had to make our way through the town. This was our final major challenge, as there were no officials to operate the locks, and they only opened twice a day. We had to wait for the afternoon shift, along with about 9 other vessels. It was quite ridiculous. There were no courtesy docks either, so we had to head towards Sète.

Upon arriving in the bustling city, we spotted a grand bridge in the distance that opened twice a day for a mere 15 minutes each time. This design was to avoid obstructing traffic in a city already grappling with severe traffic congestion issues. Unfortunately, we didn't make it in time to cross the bridge. The situation became even more complicated when a tramontana, with gusts of up to 33 knots, suddenly struck without warning, as if it were an extremely localized phenomenon that had even escaped the weather forecasts.

In the midst of this complexity, to our left, we had a pier clearly marked "no mooring," and there was no other available space. The only option was to turn back, but with that wind, we couldn't rely on sails, which we didn't have. So, we made the decision to tack the sailboat and carefully bring the bow as close as possible to the nearest concrete quay, where we could temporarily secure it. Unfortunately, at that moment, we lost two of our fenders, which literally went flying due to the intensity of the wind. It was clear that this part of the city was not prepared for navigation, especially in moments like that.

As we approached the bow, we threw a line, and fortunately, a kind person nearby was able to tie a provisional knot to secure the boat. Finally, the wind calmed enough to allow us to secure the sailboat with a total of seven fenders. With the vessel finally secure, we decided to relax and celebrate with some well-deserved beers.

We had no way to contact the bridge authorities at that time. Eventually, we found a neighbor who claimed to know the bridge's opening time, although his confidence was limited. He advised us to stay vigilant.

The next morning, we were ready to move forward. As we approached the bridge, an alarm sounded, beckoning us. With the boat prepared, we prepared to cross. However, it's worth noting that nautical charts did not provide a clear description of which bridges would open and which would not. Just after we crossed the bridge, barely five minutes later, it started to lower, and the next bridge, which we had to pass through just 400 meters away, also began to descend. Frustration overwhelmed us, and we realized we wouldn't make it in time. In just two days, we had advanced only 400 meters.

At that point, infuriated, we decided to dock in the city's harbor and seek an explanation for this apparent lack of coordination. We learned that the last bridge we hadn't crossed opened only once a day and wouldn't do so again. We were told that the city practically came to a standstill every time a bridge was raised.

However, upon learning that our goal was to reach the Mediterranean, they coordinated the opening of the remaining two bridges for the next day. As compensation for the troubles caused, they offered us a free mooring in the harbor, and the kind man who helped us with the information even offered to call a nearby port to facilitate the raising of our sailboat's mast.

At that moment, as we reflected on the incredible odyssey we had experienced, with miles behind us, a 360-meter altitude gain, three river crossings, journeys through tunnels, and the conquering of over 180 locks, we realized it was time to enjoy a well-deserved shower, explore the city, and toast with a few beers. This adventure had been quite a challenge, and we had overcome unexpected obstacles with tenacity and determination. We were practically in the Mediterranean...

The following morning, after a slight hangover, we secured all the equipment on board the sailboat as we headed for open sea.

At the agreed-upon time, we were ready, and the first bridge began to rise. Through the VHF radio, we heard the instruction to move forward, as the controllers of the other bridges were aware that they couldn't lower until we passed with the Colibrí. It was as if we were finally escaping from a cage, and we ventured into the vastness of the sea. The feeling of freedom was indescribable, even though the change in the sailboat's metacenter made it a bit unstable. However, we were determined not to let anything stop us. Our route took us to the port of D'Agde, one of the largest ports on the French Riviera. There, we planned to raise the mast and embark on another exciting adventure, which I'll soon share in detail.

This is simply a much deeper understanding of who we truly are and our authentic potential as human beings. It's a message as essential as it is universal. Know yourself. Control the beliefs you've been conditioned with by your social environment. Learn to be happy and at peace. Dare to listen to your inner voice. Discover your talents, your calling, and your purpose. Make decisions guided by your conscience and values. Follow your own path. Give your best to others. And above all, fully enjoy life...

"Who begins to live more seriously inside, starts to live more simply on the outside."

Ernest Hemingway

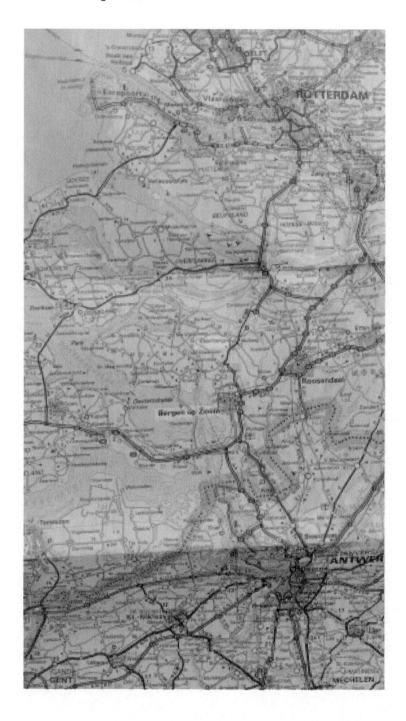

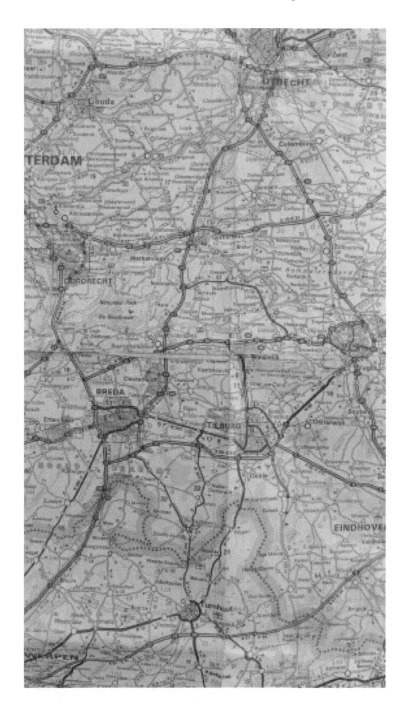

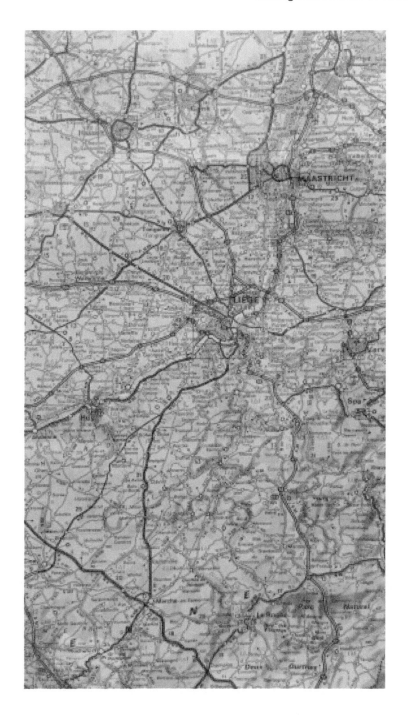

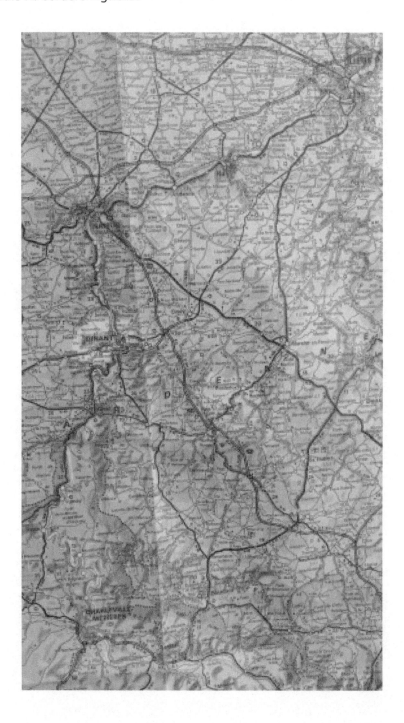

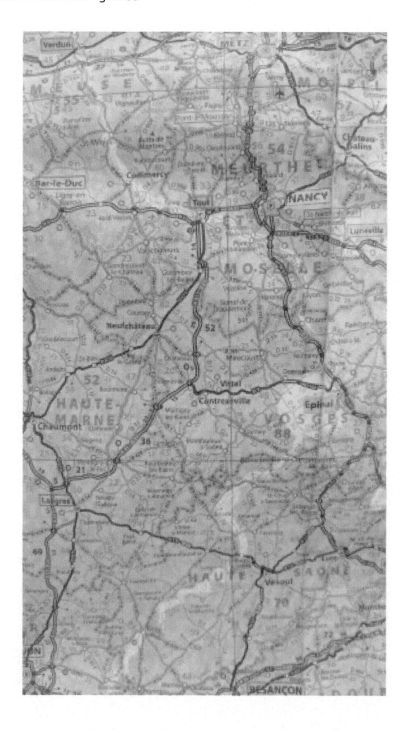

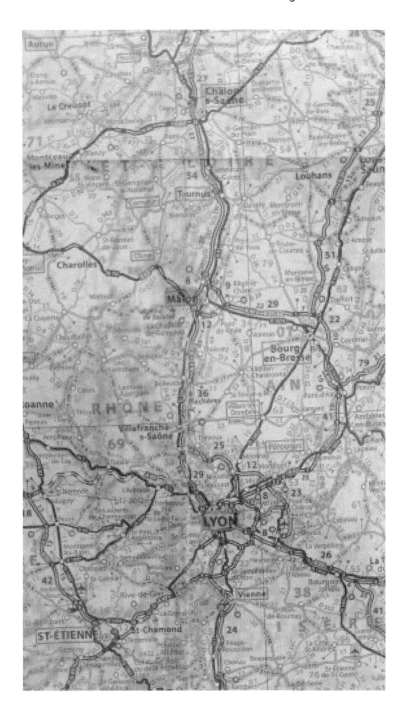

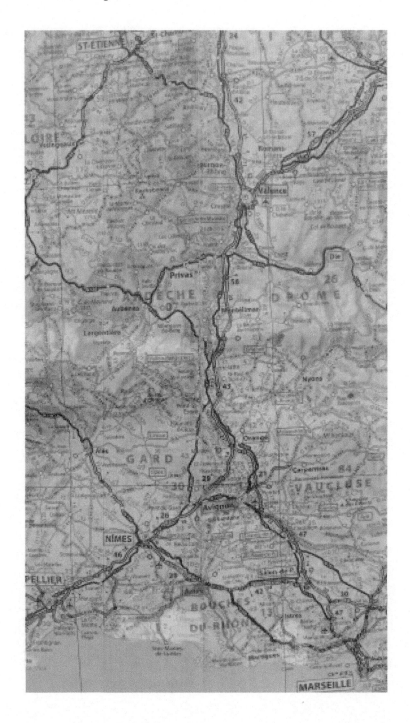

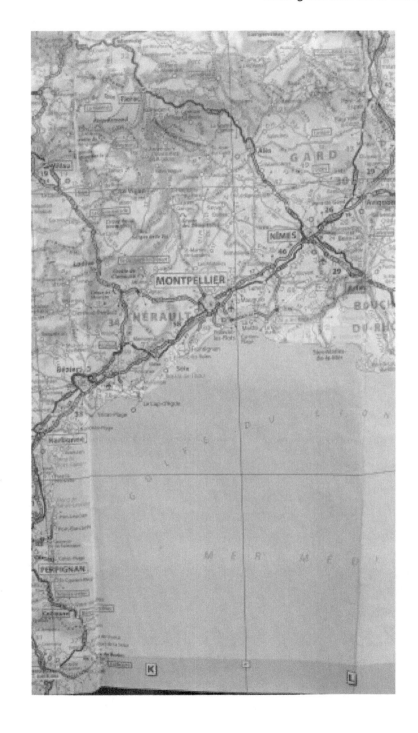

Gratitude

I express my profound gratitude to all the people who have acquired this little work, as well as to those who, on this journey, have shared their smiles, wisdom, and the simple joy of sharing with me.

I want to give special recognition to a person who has been an exceptional companion, with a generous heart that supported me in taking this leap. Thank you, Su. Also, I cannot help but thank my mother, who, despite the mistakes, has always been there and has been one of the most fervent supporters of this project. To my great friend, Beto, thank you for your support; we will soon start with our networks, hahaha! A strong hug.

Parallel to the story I share, I hope that this work serves as a role model to pursue our dreams. If someone like me has achieved such a feat, I am sure all of you can do it, try it, or simply enjoy reading it.

"I went to the seas because I wanted to live deliberately, to face only the essential facts of life, and, if I could learn what life had to teach, and not, when I came to die, discover that I had not lived."

Contact

Flickr – Gonzalo Cordero - LocoGon

Goncorderito@hotmail.com

"Without further ado, thank you very much."

Printed by Amazon Italia Logistica S.r.l.
Torrazza Piemonte (TO), Italy

52643663R00067